# What Is Electricity?

### By Lisa Trumbauer

**Consultants**
David Larwa
National Science Consultant

Nanci R. Vargus, Ed.D.
Assistant Professor of Literacy
University of Indianapolis
Indianapolis, Indiana

Children's Press®
A Division of Scholastic Inc.
New York   Toronto   London   Auckland   Sydney
Mexico City   New Delhi   Hong Kong
Danbury, Connecticut

Designer: Herman Adler Design
Photo Researcher: Caroline Anderson
The photo on the cover shows bolts of lightning.

**Library of Congress Cataloging-in-Publication Data**

Trumbauer, Lisa, 1963-
  What is electricity? / by Lisa Trumbauer.
      p. cm. — (Rookie read-about science)
Includes index.
Summary: A simple introduction to electricity, describing how it is produced
and some of the ways we use it every day.
  ISBN 0-516-23449-8 (lib. bdg.)            0-516-25845-1 (pbk.)
  1. Electricity—Juvenile literature. [1. Electricity.] I. Title. II. Series.
QC527.2.T78 2003
537—dc22
                                              2003019062

CHILDREN'S PRESS, and ROOKIE READ-ABOUT®,
and associated logos are trademarks and or registered trademarks
of Scholastic Library Publishing. SCHOLASTIC and associated logos
are trademarks and or registered trademarks of Scholastic Inc.

1 2 3 4 5 6 7 8 9 10 R 13 12 11 10 09 08 07 06 05 04

What happens when
you turn on a light?

What happens when
you turn on a computer?

You use electricity.
Electricity is a kind
of energy.

Most of the time you
cannot see electricity.

# It moves inside of wires.

When you do see electricity, it is a spark.

A spark is electricity moving through the air.

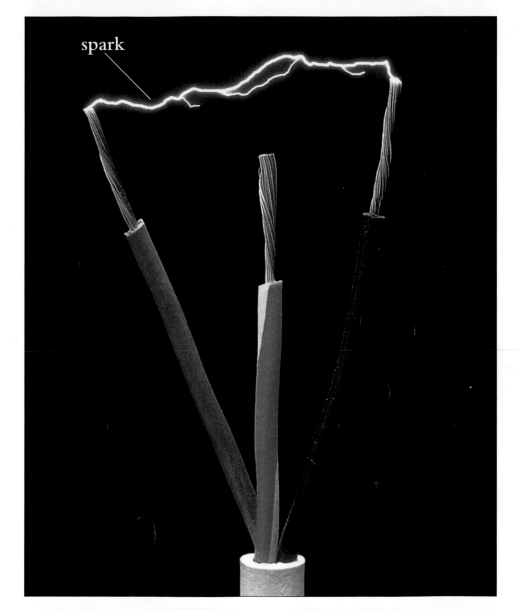

spark

Lightning is also electricity that you can see.

Lightning is electricity jumping from the clouds to the ground.

Where does the electricity
in your home come from?
It comes from a power plant.

These power plants can be
far from your house.

Power plant

The electricity gets from the power plant to your house through wires.

Big wires called cables are connected to the power plant.

Some cables are high
up on poles. Some
are underground.

A cable goes from the
street into your house. It
connects to smaller wires
inside the walls.

When you plug something in, the plug connects to the wires in the wall.

These wires are hooked up to other wires that go all the way to the power plant.

Now, electricity can move through the wire.

Light bulbs were one of the first things to be run by electricity.

A light bulb glows when electricity moves through a wire and heats it up.

The electricity can make things move. Electricity makes fans turn.

Toy trains run because
of electricity.

Not all electricity comes from a power plant.

Sometimes it comes from a battery. The first batteries were very large.

Batteries became smaller
and easier to use. Today, we
put batteries in many things.

Watches have batteries. Some radios have batteries, too.

You use electricity all
the time.

Turn on a light. Start up
your computer. Play a
video game.

You are using electricity.

# Words You Know

batteries

cable

computer

lightning

power plant

spark

# Index

# About the Author

Lisa Trumbauer has written a dozen books about the physical sciences and dozens more about other branches of science. She has also edited science programs for teachers of young children. Lisa lives in New Jersey with one dog, two cats, and her husband, Dave.

# Photo Credits

Photographs © 2004: Corbis Images: 25 (Archivo Iconografico, S.A.), 23 (William Gottlieb), 29 (Jose Luis Pelaez, Inc.), 18, 22 (Royalty-Free); Corbis Sygma/Bernard Annebicque: 26, 30 top; Photo Researchers, NY: 13, 31 bottom left (Ted Clutter), 9, 31 bottom right (Victor De Schwanberg); PhotoEdit: 7 (Tony Freeman), 27 (Michael Newman), 4, 21, 30 bottom right (David Young-Wolff); PictureQuest: 10, 31 top (Corbis Images), 3 (Stockbyte); The Image Works: 17, 30 bottom left (Dorothy Littell Greco), 14 (Thelma Shumsky); Visuals Unlimited: cover (Charles A. Doswell III), 6 (Bernd Wittich).